Development of Science and Technology in Islamic History

Shabeer Ahmad

مكتبة

مكتبة

مكتبة   مكتبة اسلامية   Maktabaslamia

MaktabaIslamia Publications

www.maktabaislamia.com
info@maktabaislamia.com
www.facebook.com/everythingislamic
www.twitter.com/maktabaislamia

2016 CE – 1437 H

Translation of the Qur'ān

It should be perfectly clear that the Qur'ān is only authentic in its original language, Arabic. Since perfect translation of the Qur'ān is impossible, we have used the translation of the meaning of the Qur'ān throughout the book, as the result is only a crude meaning of the Arabic text.

Qur'ānic verses appear in speech marks proceeded by a reference to the Surah and verse number. Sayings (*Hadith*) of Prophet Muhammad ﷺ appear in inverted commas along with reference to the Hadith Book and its Reporter.

صلى الله عليه وسلم - ﷺ (Peace be upon him)

سبحانه وتعالى - ﷻ (Glory to Him, the Exalted)

Table of Contents

"800 years of invention and prosperity"

"...I'll end by telling a story. There was once a civilization that was the greatest in the world.

It was able to create a continental super-state that stretched from ocean to ocean, and from northern climes to tropics and deserts. Within its dominion lived hundreds of millions of people, of different creeds and ethnic origins.

One of its languages became the universal language of much of the world, the bridge between the peoples of a hundred lands. Its armies were made up of people of many nationalities, and its military protection allowed a degree of peace and prosperity that had never been known. The reach of this civilization's commerce extended from Latin America to China, and everywhere in between.

And this civilization was driven more than anything, by invention. Its architects designed buildings that defied gravity. Its mathematicians created the algebra and algorithms that would enable the building of computers, and the creation of encryption. Its doctors examined the human body, and found new cures for disease. Its astronomers looked into the heavens, named the stars, and paved the way for space travel and exploration.

Its writers created thousands of stories. Stories of courage, romance and magic. Its poets wrote of love, when others before them were too steeped in fear to think of such things.

When other nations were afraid of ideas, this civilization thrived on them, and kept them alive. When censors threatened to wipe out knowledge from past civilizations, this civilization kept the knowledge alive, and passed it on to others.

While modern Western civilization shares many of these traits, the civilization I'm talking about was the Islamic world from the year 800 to 1600, which included the Ottoman Empire and the courts of Baghdad, Damascus and Cairo, and enlightened rulers like Suleiman the Magnificent.

Although we are often unaware of our indebtedness to this other civilization, its gifts are very much a part of our heritage. The technology industry would not exist without the contributions of Arab mathematicians. Sufi poet-philosophers like Rumi challenged our notions of self and truth. Leaders like Suleiman contributed to our notions of tolerance and civic leadership.

And perhaps we can learn a lesson from his example: It was leadership based on meritocracy, not inheritance. It was leadership that harnessed the full capabilities of a very diverse population-that included Christianity, Islamic, and Jewish traditions.

This kind of enlightened leadership - leadership that nurtured culture, sustainability, diversity and courage - led to 800 years of invention and prosperity..."

Carly Fiorina, former CEO of Hewlett-Packard, 26 September 2001.

Introduction

In the last 300 years Europe has contributed immensely to the universal knowledge of science and technology. Tribute must be paid to the countless individuals for their outstanding work. The sheer dedication and devotion to science in Europe was second to none, and the world is in debt to this enormous contribution.

Many of European scientist's life and work have been scrutinized and documented in the annals of history. Their staggering contribution to science can be seen from the names of laws of sciences, inventions and recent discoveries. For example, Newton's Laws are universally known, as are the words Volts and Watts, which come from the names of the great European scientists Sir Isaaq Newton, Alessandro Volta and James Watt.

It is therefore not surprising that people often view Europe as the birthplace of science and technology. The implication of this viewpoint is that modern scientific age is exclusively the endeavor of the European nations. Many books of history point to the European scientists, like Galileo and Newton, as the fathers of modern sciences, thus reinforcing the view that Europe is the birth place of science and technology.

In the absence of any historical context, the uneducated reader can be forgiven for having a narrow view that Europe is origin of science and technology. Based on an objective study of history, it can be seen that the huge strides made in Europe in science and technology did not happen in a vacuum. Europe did not suddenly wake up one day and decided to embark on a road of scientific discoveries, as is commonly portrayed. In fact, there were two enablers that thrust Europe ahead of others in science and technology in a short period of time:

- Adoption of Capitalistic ideology

7

- Access to 1000 years of scientific heritage

As for adoption of an ideology, Europeans divorced Christianity from the state, and adopted Capitalism[1] as an ideology. This led to a unified vision of life, liberation in thinking, adoption of common framework for solving problems, accountability and guaranteed rights for individuals.

Furthermore, Europe had access to a millennium of rich scientific heritage. This proved invaluable for kick starting the industrial revolution, thus it became the bedrock on which Europe took the leadership in the field of science and technology.

Whose millennium of scientific heritage did Europe use? This is the fundamental question that is never answered clearly. Much is taught in Europe about the Greeks and the Romans, and then there is a leap in history to the modern times. 1000 years of history is simply lost in the middle as though this period was insignificant to mankind. This lost history is none other than the history of Islam, in which the citizens of the Islamic State led the world in many fields of human activity. The rich scientific heritage is none other than the Islamic scientific heritage that was the product of the Islamic System. In this period of 1000 years, Islam dominated and led much of the civilized world.

No mention is made of the fact that great deal of European scientific heritage actually came from the Muslims, who not only extended Greek, Persian and India works, but they were also pioneers themselves, contributing immensely to sciences. They laid foundation of various sciences though discovering laws, establishing principles and formalizing scientific thinking. It is this treasure that the West used as a springboard, yet little credit is given to Islam and the Muslims.

---

[1] Capitalism is not only a definition of an economic system based on the free market principles, but it is also used as definition of a way of life where religion is separated from the running of the state and man becomes sovereign i.e. man has the right to legislate. In this way of life, capitalistic economic system is the most prominent system in society.

Furthermore, the West has always claimed that its scientific progress was a direct result of separating religion from the practical life of the people, in other words, separating the Church from the State. It is stated that religion cannot deal with the man's affairs in the ever changing modern world, and adopting it only stifles creativity and progress in many walks of life, including science and technology.

It is a fact that throughout the history of Europe, the Church was engaged in harsh treatment of the people, especially the scientists and the thinkers who opposed the views of the Church. This stagnated scientific thought and as a result, religion was perceived as impractical, inflexible, and full of contradictions. Hence, it was found to be unsuitable for the progress of humanity.

The Europeans have indeed suffered greatly under the Church. However, can generalizations be made, based on the experience of Christianity in Europe, that progress can only be made through man-made legislations and that Divine Revelation is somewhat inadequate or defective? Can this analogy also be applied to Islam? Did Islam stifle development of science and technology? Is there a contradiction between science and Islam?

This book has two main objectives:

1. To examine the argument that there is a contradiction between science and Islam. This argument originates from European experience of Christianity but it universally applied to include all religions nowadays.
2. To highlight some of the great contributions made by Muslims to science and technology over a period of 1000 years. This scientific heritage of the Muslims formed the basis of European scientific revolution.

The book is structured in two parts:

Part 1 deals with the first objective mentioned above. It begins by tracing the historical roots of the European argument that science and religion are contradictory. It then goes to show that there is no contradiction between scientific discovery and Islam, as Islam is a way of life and not merely a set of rules related to worships devoid of reality.

Part 2 begins by showing the motivating factors that led to advances in science and technology amongst the Muslims, and then it highlights the contributions made by the scientist to various disciples like mathematic, chemistry and so on. A list of leading scientists of the Islamic State, from the beginning of the Islamic rule in 622 CE to its end in 1924 CE, is also presented. Lastly, the factors that led to the decline of scientific thought in the Islamic State are highlighted, and Appendices provide useful quotes about Muslim scientists and the Arabic origins of many words used today in the English language.

PART 1

The Dark Ages in Europe

The adoption of Christianity by the Roman Empire was not based on the truthfulness of Christianity or on its ability to deal with man's problems. Rather, it was adopted by Constantine in 325 Christian Era (CE) to simply preserve the empire by building a common mentality and loyalty among the citizens. Christianity offered blind loyalty to the secular emperors, based on the understanding that the temporal authority and the spiritual authority can harmoniously co-exist.

This understanding came from the saying attributed to Jesus,

> "Render unto Caesar what is Caesar's and unto God what is God's."

Despite this, Christianity could not preserve the empire, and the demise of the Romans bequeathed many Christian states in Europe where the Church was able to dominate.

The domination of the Church meant that all affairs of life had to conform to the dogma of the Church. This caused many problems because the Bible, which the Church used as its authoritative text, dealt with only very limited matters. It gave some specific rules related to worships and foodstuffs. It gave general moral principles for Christians and set norms for their prayers and communal worship. Unlike the legislative sources of Islam, the Bible does not give detailed guidance on economy, politics, judiciary, criminal punishments, the structure and functioning of government and so on. The Qur'an informs that the Christians and Jews had changed their books so the Bible does not represent a preserved text from the Creator to man, and it leaves a huge gap when it comes to human societal affairs. This gap was an area of constant conflict of interests between kings, feudal barons and priests. During Europe's dark ages it was the priests who dominated life and when they gave judgments even kings had to submit. Yet these judgments of priests were an arbitrary and inconsistent exercise of their authority owing to the lack of a comprehensive legislative text to base their rules upon, and this laid the seeds of direct confrontation between the society and the Church.

With the passage of time, scientific discoveries were made that were at odds with the teachings of the Church. To preserve its authority, the Church took some harsh steps against the emergence of new ideas. Many scientists were branded as heretics, infidels and satans. In 1042 AH/ 1633 CE, Galileo was forced to renounce his belief and writings that supported the Copernican theory of heliocentrism that claimed the sun was the center of the universe. Instead, the Church adamantly maintained the flawed theory of geocentrism, which stated that the earth was the center of the universe.

Also, plenty of evidence exists indicating that tens of thousands of women, who were alleged to be witches, were burnt or drowned. The response to this oppression from the people, especially the scientists, thinkers, and the philosophers such as Voltaire and Rousseau, was equally strong. They began to highlight the contradictions of the Church and called for nothing less than the separation of the Church and the State. The struggle had begun.

Desperate measures were taken by the Church to deflect the criticism, frustration and anger that were vented by the people. These measures failed to halt the flames of change that had galvanized the masses. The Church realized that it could no longer stay in charge of the State without reforming itself. Thus, a period of Reformation commenced. However, the Reformation did not guarantee any bright future for the Church as the struggle became intensified between the 16th and the 17th century CE.

The eventual outcome of the struggle for power between the Church and the thinkers and philosophers was the separation of the Church and the

State. This solution was a compromise that limited the authority of the Church to preserving the morals in society and conducting rituals, and left the administration of the worldly affairs to the State. The separation between the Church and the State through the compromise solution was completed by the 18th century CE, and formed the basis of Capitalism, marking the beginning of the Enlightenment period that sparked the industrial revolution in Europe.

It is therefore clear that Europe stagnated scientifically under the arbitrary authority of the Christian Church.

Islam as an Ideology

In order to understand the relationship between science and Islam, it is necessary first to explain Islam, as it was Islam that provided the driving force of change and research in science. It is the Islamic ideology that deserves the credit and not just the individuals only.

The word 'Islam', in Arabic, linguistically means submission. As a term, 'Islam' refers to the Message that was revealed to Muhammad (saw[2]) by Allah, the One Creator, and a 'Muslim' is the one who believes in Allah, and accepts Muhammad (saw) as the last and final Prophet and Messenger of Allah. Consequently, a Muslim believes in Islam in its entirety.

In sharp contrast to Christianity and Judaism, Islam is not merely a religion. Rather, Islam is a unique and comprehensive ideology that guides the life of the human being. The Islamic ideology, by the definition of an ideology, consists of both the 'Aqeedah (creed, doctrine) and Systems, to regulate the practical life of human beings.

The Islamic 'Aqeedah provides the correct and comprehensive answers to the fundamental questions regarding humanity's existence and that of the universe. It addresses the issue of the human being's purpose in life, and links it with what preceded life and what will come after it, thereby settling humanity's core problem and providing the basis for systems and rules to properly organize human affairs. This 'Aqeedah also provides the basis for a means to implement Islam in reality, thus transferring it from 'theory' to 'practice'. This means of implementing Islam is through the State. The State is an integral part of the ideology and distinguishes it from a philosophy, which provides hypothetical ideas but no means to implement them.

---

[2] saw – *sallallah alayhim wa sallam* (may peace be upon him). This is always used whenever the name of Prophet Muhammad is used as a mark of respect.

14

Islam provide a comprehensive structure to govern the affairs of human beings. It correctly establishes:

1) The relationship between the human being and his Creator
2) The personal affairs of individuals
3) The various relationships (social, political, economic, and international) that exist in the society

Thus, Islam constitutes a Creed and Systems. What distinguishes Islam from the ideologies of Capitalism and Communism is that Islam is built on the correct idea, whereas the others are founded on a shallow and unenlightened view of the life of the human being and the world in which he exists.

Because Islam establishes the correct understanding of life and places humanity in the correct context, the systems and culture emanating from the Islamic creed would correctly address the human nature and provide the correct solutions. In this context, Islam is compatible with the human being. Islam does not ignore a human being's instincts or desires, but organizes them in the proper context, including the survival instinct that prompts man to seek material progress through the acquisition of science and technology.

Islam is an ideology that was revealed to the world. The spread of Islam is neither confined to time or place, nor dependent upon science and technology. Although science and technology has changed the living conditions of the people around the globe, the needs and instincts of humanity have not changed. Therefore, Islam, which came to organize the needs and instincts through its implementation upon society, is applicable and valid for all time.

Relationship between Science and Islam

Islam is a system of life that originated from the Allah, the Creator. Allah is the One who created man, life, and the universe and subjected man to the physical laws that He imposed on the universe. The Qur'an, as revealed to Muhammad (saw), directs man to think and study the physical world in order to understand the reality and to appreciate more the greatness of the Creator.

Many verses in the Qur'an point to the physical world and explain natural phenomena, as a confirmation for humanity that this revelation came from the Creator. Some of these explanations could not be understood at the time of the revelation because mankind did not have the tools that are taken for granted in modern times, such as the microscope, X-rays and so on. It is only during the last hundred years that some of these explanations became understood as a result of advances in science.

The examples in the Qur'an are many and range from the creation of the universe down to the fertilization of the egg by the sperm. It will suffice here just to quote few of these verses.

إِنَّ فِي خَلْقِ السَّمَاوَاتِ وَالأَرْضِ وَاخْتِلاَفِ اللَّيْلِ وَالنَّهَارِ وَالْفُلْكِ الَّتِي تَجْرِي فِي الْبَحْرِ بِمَا يَنفَعُ النَّاسَ وَمَا أَنزَلَ اللّهُ مِنَ السَّمَاء مِن مَّاء فَأَحْيَا بِهِ الأَرْضَ بَعْدَ مَوْتِهَا وَبَثَّ فِيهَا مِن كُلِّ دَآبَّةٍ وَتَصْرِيفِ الرِّيَاحِ وَالسَّحَابِ الْمُسَخِّرِ بَيْنَ السَّمَاء وَالأَرْضِ لآيَاتٍ لِّقَوْمٍ يَعْقِلُونَ

"Verily! In the creation of the heavens and the earth, and in the alternation of night and day, and the ships which sail through the sea with that which is of use to mankind, and the rain which Allah sends down from the sky and makes the earth alive therewith after its death, and the moving (living) creatures of all kinds that He scatters therein, and in the veering of winds and clouds which are held between the sky and the earth, are indeed proofs for people of understanding." [Translation of the meaning of the

16

Qur'an, 2:164]

And,

وَإِنَّ لَكُمْ فِي الْأَنْعَامِ لَعِبْرَةً نُّسْقِيكُم مِّمَّا فِي بُطُونِهِ مِن بَيْنِ فَرْثٍ وَدَمٍ لَّبَنًا خَالِصًا سَآئِغًا لِلشَّارِبِينَ

"Verily, in cattle there is a lesson for you. We give you to drink of what is inside their bodies, coming from a conjunction between the contents of the intestines and blood, a milk pure and pleasant for those who drink it." [Translation of the meaning of the Qur'an, 16:66]

And,

أَلَمْ تَرَ أَنَّ اللَّهَ سَخَّرَ لَكُم مَّا فِي الْأَرْضِ وَالْفُلْكَ تَجْرِي فِي الْبَحْرِ بِأَمْرِهِ وَيُمْسِكُ السَّمَاء أَن تَقَعَ عَلَى الْأَرْضِ إِلَّا بِإِذْنِهِ إِنَّ اللَّهَ بِالنَّاسِ لَرَؤُوفٌ رَّحِيمٌ

"Do you not see that Allah has made subservient to you whatsoever is in the earth, and the ships that sail through the sea by His command? He withholds the heaven from falling on the earth except by His Leave. Verily, Allah is, for mankind, full of Kindness, Most Merciful." [Translation of the meaning of the Qur'an, 22:65]

And,

ثُمَّ جَعَلْنَاهُ نُطْفَةً فِي قَرَارٍ مَّكِينٍ- ثُمَّ خَلَقْنَا النُّطْفَةَ عَلَقَةً فَخَلَقْنَا الْعَلَقَةَ مُضْغَةً فَخَلَقْنَا الْمُضْغَةَ عِظَامًا فَكَسَوْنَا الْعِظَامَ لَحْمًا ثُمَّ أَنشَأْنَاهُ خَلْقًا آخَرَ فَتَبَارَكَ اللَّهُ أَحْسَنُ الْخَالِقِينَ - ثُمَّ إِنَّكُمْ بَعْدَ ذَلِكَ لَمَيِّتُونَ

"Then We placed him as (a drop of) sperm in a place of rest, firmly fixed. Then we made the sperm into a thing which clings (to the womb), then of that thing We made a (fetus) lump, then We made out of that lump, bones and clothed the bones with flesh,

17

then We developed out of it another creature. So blessed be Allah, the perfect Creator."
[Translation of the meaning of the Qur'an, 23:13-14]

Although Qur'an points to the physical world to make people think, and it encourages people to discover physical laws, the Qur'an is not a book of science. Rather, it came to organize human relationships with the self, with other humans, with the Creator, and with the surroundings. Islamic law therefore deals with the proper use of scientific facts and not with their discovery. For example, Islam does not prevent people from designing a space craft or a laser gun, but it does lay down principles for their use.

Evidence that Islam does not interfere with scientific discovery can be seen from an incident that took place during the time of the Messenger of Allah (saw), who once suggested to farmers that it might be better if they left palm date trees without cross-pollinating them as they did every year. The following year, farmers complained that the trees did not produce normal yield, so the Messenger of Allah (saw) said, "You know the affairs of your world better." This means that this advice was not from Islamic text; rather it was a personal opinion of the Messenger of Allah (saw) as a man. Thus, people were left to their own scientific discovery and applications.   [ ] = important

Also, there are no records in history to show that the Islamic State, its scholars or learned people ever gave Islamic rulings on scientific matters, unlike the Church in Europe which interfered with scientific discovery. In fact, many of the leading scientists were also Islamic scholars, and they did not see any contradiction between science and Islam. However, few scientists went beyond their subject matters and propagated incorrect ideas about Islamic belief, for which they were rebuked and corrected but not tortured or persecuted.

There is, therefore, no contradiction between Islam and science.

18

PART 2

Factors for scientific advancement in Islamic History

The notion that religion is at odds with scientific development is alien to Islam. History shows that most of the scientific developments by the Muslims and non-Muslim citizens were achieved under the rule of Islam, and not by coincidence, haphazardly or when Islam was removed from practical life.

What was the motivation of the citizens to study sciences and become the founding fathers of these disciplines? What drove the citizens of the Islamic State to excel in various scientific fields? Were these people rich who had time to study and ponder; were they looking for fame and glory or were they motivated by wealth or greed?

An objective study of history shows that the main motivating factors for scientific development came from the Islamic State's policy, and not from the individuals' initiatives alone. The Khulafa[3] understood that Islam had given them two main obligations:

1. To look after the affairs of the citizens
2. To provide security for citizens against external threats

As for looking after the affairs of the citizens, this is specified in what the Messenger of Allah (saw) said, "Each of you is a shepherd and each of you is responsible for his flock. The leader is a shepherd and is responsible for his flock." [Reported in books of Bukhari and Muslim] This narration, in addition to many other evidences from Qur'an and the Sunnah, establishes the responsibility of looking after the affairs of the people on the shoulders of the Khaleefah. Looking after the affairs of the people means

---

[3] Plural for Khaleefah, or Caliph in English. Khaleefah is the title for the head of the Islamic State.

that the State must provide basic needs, security and rights, and solve problems and disputes that arise in society.

As the Islamic State expanded, its citizens and lands under its management became vast. This brought complex problems in relations to inheritance, land divisions, finances, *zakat* and booty distribution, construction, agriculture, navigation and provision of medical care. So the Khulafa' needed a systematic way to resolve these problems as part of looking after the affairs of the peoples, hence they sanctioned the development of science and technology. This is proven by what is stated by al-Khawarizmi, in his book *Al-Kitab al-Mukhtasur fi Hisab al-Jabr wa al-Muqabala*:

> "That fondness for science, by which God has distinguished the Imam al-Mamun, the Commander of the Faithful…has encouraged me to compose a short work on Calculating by (the rules of) Completion and Reduction confining it to what is easiest and most useful in arithmetic, such as men constantly require in cases of inheritance, legacies, partition, law-suits, and trade, and in all their dealings with one another, or where the measuring of lands, the digging of canals, geometrical computation, and other objects of various sorts and kinds are concerned."

As for providing security against external threats, this is achieved by preparing a powerful force to act as a deterrent against the enemies of Islam. This preparation has been made an obligation in the Qur'an,

وَأَعِدُّواْ لَهُم مَّا اسْتَطَعْتُم مِّن قُوَّةٍ وَمِن رِّبَاطِ الْخَيْلِ تُرْهِبُونَ بِهِ عَدْوَّ اللَّهِ وَعَدُوَّكُمْ وَآخَرِينَ مِن دُونِهِمْ لاَ تَعْلَمُونَهُمُ اللَّهُ يَعْلَمُهُمْ سَبِيلِ اللَّهِ يُوَفَّ إِلَيْكُمْ وَأَنتُمْ لاَ تُظْلَمُونَ

"Against them make ready your strength to the utmost of your power, including steeds of war, to strike terror into (the hearts of) the enemies, of Allah and your enemies, and others besides, whom ye may not know, but whom Allah doth know." [Translation of the meaning of the Qur'an 8:60]

20

Preparation here indicated material strength, so scientific knowledge was required to develop superior weapons that would deter the enemies of Islam, hence, there was a need to study and develop science and technology for the sake of security.

[handwritten: what does this word mean?]

Additional impetus for scientific development, especially in medicine and chemistry, came from what Abu Hurayrah narrated that Messenger of Allah (saw) said, "There is no disease that Allah has created, except that He also has created its cure." [Reported in the book of Bukhari]

[handwritten: (except for one, namely old-age)]

And, 'Usamah ibn Shuraik narrated, " 'O Allah's Messenger! Should we seek medical treatment for our illnesses?' He (saw) replied: 'Yes, you should seek medical treatment, because Allah, the Exalted, has let no disease exist without providing for its cure, except for one ailment, namely, old age'." [Reported in the book of Tirmidhi]

Thus it was clear for scientists and medical practitioners that cures were available for every disease, so they made effort in finding these cures.

It can be concluded that early Muslims and non-Muslim citizens progressed very fast in all fields of science known at the time, and pioneered into the new fields, under the supervision of the Islamic State. The Islamic State provided financial and material support for its citizens, welcomed scientists who were being persecuted by the Romans and allowed unhindered scientific research for the sake of solving practical problems. The State, therefore, created an environment in which its citizens studied, researched and developed solutions without fear or repression.

The 'Abbasi Khulafa' can be credited with providing the greatest push for the development of science and technology. They established centers of learning, like Bayt al-Hikmah in 832 CE in Baghdad, which was entrusted with the task of translating works from Greek and Sanskrit into Arabic. The Abbasids brought together some of finest thinkers, scholars and scientists of the time, and encouraged others to study and achieve high quality of work.

Glimpses of Scientific Achievements in Islamic History

The staggering contribution of Muslims and non-Muslim citizens to science and technology, as mentioned in this section, are meant only to serve as examples and should be understood as merely representative of the glorious services rendered by them to the overall development of universal science and technology. Although much of the earlier scientific knowledge of Muslims came from the Indians, Persians, Chinese and the Greeks, they rapidly extended this knowledge and established their own disciplines thereafter.

Before Islam, Arabs had a rudimentary knowledge of history and geography. Their history was limited to the annals of the local tribes and territories.

From the early days of Islam, the Muslims of all regions in general, and those of Arabian Peninsular in particular, traveled extensively through plains, hills, rivers, oceans, forests and deserts in connections with Jihad, Hajj and trade. In the course of their life they collected information on social, political, historical, geographical, economical, agricultural and other conditions of the land they visited or settled in.

As a consequence of the collection of such information, and the drive by the Islamic State for study and research, sciences such as history and geography became rich. During those days the travel was tedious and hazardous because there were no mechanical means of transportation, only animals, and no regular roads existed, yet the citizens traveled extensively through all kinds of terrain.

So far as the physical or experimental sciences are concerned, the pre-Islamic Arabs had some knowledge of them. With their keen sense of observation, they gathered information on animals like horses, camels and sheep and on the indigenous plants of their vast deserts. Some medical use of these plants was also known to them. The names mentioned in the pre-

Islamic Arabic literature of various internal and external organs of the human and animal bodies suggest that their knowledge of anatomy was quite fair. The Arabs had some knowledge of astronomy and meteorology as well. They had some information on the fixed stars, the movements of the planets and the patterns of weather. A number of arts and crafts such as horse breeding and camel rearing were also in existence among them.

In order to make the foreign scientific works easily understandable, it was necessary to undertake the selective translations of these scientific works into Arabic. Arabic, being a flexible and rich language, easily provided sufficient terminology for the new sciences. The objective was not just to translate but rather to build upon what was translated.

A number of academies were established in many places in the Muslim world to carry out the work of translation. During the rule of the 'Abbasi Khulafa', particularly al-Mansur (754 – 775 CE) and al-Ma'mun (813 – 833 CE), extensive activity was shown in the preparation and translation of scientific works. One such example is the establishment of Bayt al-Hikmah (House of Wisdom) in 832 CE in Baghdad, which acted as the central repository of translated work in Arabic. ⤳ Iraq

Significant work was accomplished by the end of the 10th century CE. The translators belonged to different ethnic and religious groups. For instance, Nawbakht was of Persian origin. Muhammad ibn Ibrahim al-Fazari was an Arab. Hunayn ibn Ishaq was a Nestorian Christian from Hirah[4].

The Muslim scientists accepted the scientific conclusions of others subject to their experimental verification and also made new observations and experiments that lead to new discoveries. Muslim scientists used the practical approach to scientific problems with the abstract thought.

---

[4] An ancient city located south of Kufah, Iraq. It was prominent in pre-Islamic Arab history.

24

Muslim scientists recognized the physical or qualitative and the mathematical or quantitative aspects of science. They made qualitative as well as quantitative studies of numerous scientific problems. For instance, Ibn Khurdad-bih determined the latitudes and longitudes of various places in the Muslim world. Al-Biruni ascertained the specific gravity of a number of substances.

The experiments in chemistry, physics and medicine were performed in the laboratories and those in pathology and surgery in the hospitals. Observatories were set up at various places in the Muslim world, such as Damascus, Baghdad, and Nishapur[5] to perform astronomical observations.

Arrangements for the dissection of the corpses were made for the practical teaching of anatomy. The Khaleefah al-Mu'tasim (833 – 842 CE) supplied a physician with apes for this purpose. Practical demonstrations of surgical operations for the students were given in the hospitals.

Literacy had reached the highest standard among the Muslim people during the 11th and 12th century CE. The scientific spirit of that age is indicated by the optical work of Shihab al-Din al-Qarafi, a scholar of *fiqh* and judge of Cairo, which dealt with fifty optical problems.

In Islamic State, scientists not only made original contributions to science but also applied their scientific discoveries in technological innovation. They observed the stars, and prepared star maps for navigational purposes. Ibn Yunus made use of pendulum for the measurement of time. Ibn Sina used air thermometers to measure air temperature. Paper, compass, gun, gunpowder, inorganic acids and alkaline bases are some of the most important examples of scientific and technological developments of Muslim scientists, which brought about an unprecedented revolution in

---

[5] A city in the Razavi Khorasan province in northeastern Iran.

human civilization.

Muslim scientists made algebra a permanent branch of mathematics. The word 'algebra' is derived from its original Arabic root *jabr*. Muslim scientists also evolved plane and spherical trigonometry, and applied it to astronomy. They also separated astrology from astronomy, because a belief in the influence of stars on the fate of human beings is heresy in Islam. Astronomy was thus developed to the stage of a pure science after its purification from superstitious beliefs.

The numerous Arabic words and scientific terms currently being used in European languages are living monuments of Muslim contributions to modern science. In addition, the large number of books in the libraries of Asia and Europe, the museums of many countries, and the mosques and palaces built centuries ago also bear an eloquent testimony to this important phenomenon of world history.

Some examples of words derived from Arabic are: cipher and chiffre (in English and French respectively), derived from the Arabic word *sifr* (meaning empty or nil), describing a number written at the right of another numeral to increase its value ten times; the word alkali in chemical terminology used for that particular substance which gives a salt when combined with an acid, is a modified form of the Arabic word *al-qali*; the French word escadre and the English word squadron for a section of armed forces, have been derived form the Arabic word *'askariyyah* used in the same sense; and the word admiral is derived from *amir al-rahl* and there are many others.

In the process of translation, the names of a large number of Muslim scholars have also altered, deceiving readers into thinking that they are the names of non-Muslim Europeans. Some such names are: Abu al-Qasim al-Zahrawi is known as Albucasis, Muhammad ibn Jabir ibn Sinan al-Battani is known as Albetinius and Abu 'Ali ibn Sina is known as Avicenna.

It is quite obvious that the spirit of inquiry created in the Muslims and the scientific method of investigation that they formulated resulted in the evolution of modern science.

Mathematics

- Number Zero
- Arabic Numbers
- Algorithms
- Al-Khwarizmi's Work on Algebra
- Spherical, Analytical & Plane Trigonometry
- Determining Roots of Quadratic Equation
- Sine, Cosine Tables
- Cubic Equations
- Work of Banu Musa on Geometry

The achievements of Muslims in the field of mathematics are extremely remarkable, and they laid the foundations on which the Western mathematics developed many centuries later.

During the 11th century CE nearly all of the original and creative work was done by Muslims. Arabic became the language in which all work was written, and even non-Muslims wrote their mathematical works in Arabic.

Extending the ancient Indian numbering system, the Muslims used numbers including the zero for counting in contrast with writing the amounts in words or counting with the letters of the alphabet. Thus they made arithmetic simple and applicable to the problems of everyday life in connection with commerce and trade. The number zero holds great importance in arithmetic. Without the zero it is not possible to indicate the figure like tens, hundreds and so on.

The West learned the use of numerals from the Muslims, and naturally, called them the Arabic numerals. The diffusion of the Arabic numerals in Christian Europe was, however, slow. The Christian mathematicians either used the old Roman numerals and the abacus, or used the Arabic numerals together with their old system.

The symbols used today for numbers in the West are derived from the Arabic symbols.

It was only in the 12th century CE that after learning from the Muslims the Western scholars were able to produce some literature on the number system without columns and incorporating the zero. This system was named algorithms (or algorism) which was derived by the Latin writers from al-Khwarizmi[6], a distinguished Muslim mathematicians, astronomer and geographer of the 9th century CE who flourished under the Khaleefah al-Ma'mun. His full name was Abu 'Abdullah Muhammad ibn Musa al-Khwarizmi (d. 850 CE). His influence on mathematical thought exceeded that of any other writer of that period. He wrote an encyclopedic work dealing with arithmetic, geometry, music and astronomy.

Algebra was made into an exact science by the Muslims. Al-Khwarizmi named his book dealing with this subject as *Al-Kitab al-Mukhtasur fi Hisab al-Jabr wa al-Muqabala* (The Book of Restitution and Comparison). The word *jabr* means restitution. It is the adding of some thing to a given sum or multiplying it so that it becomes equal to another value. The word *muqabalah* means comparison and is applied in comparing two sides of an equation such as A+B = C. The word *al-jabr* (Algebra) was originally used for simple operations, like additions and multiplication, but later it evolved into an entire subject. He is rightly considered the father of algebra.

The equations described by Khwarizmi were word based and he did not use any symbols in formulating the algebraic equations and their solutions, as it is common today. The following is a sample from his book *Al-Kitab al-Mukhtasur fi Hisab al-Jabr wa al-Muqabala*:

"Roots and Squares are equal to Numbers;2 for instance, "one

---

[6] A native of Khwarizm region, now called Khiva on river Amu Darya, south of the Aral Sea in what is now Uzbekistan.

square, and ten roots of the same, amount to thirty-nine dirhems;" that is to say, what must be the square which, when increased by ten of its own roots, amount to thirty-nine? The solution is this: you halve the number of the roots, which in the present instance yields five. This you multiply by itself; the product is twenty-five. Add this to thirty-nine; the sum is sixty-four. Now take the root of this, which is eight, and subtract from it half the number of the roots, which is five; the remainder is three. This is the root of the square which you sought for; the square itself is nine."

In addition, the Muslims founded analytical geometry as well as plane and spherical trigonometry.

Al-Hajjaj ibn Yusuf ibn Matar, who flourished between 786 CE and 833 CE in Baghdad, was the first to translate Euclid's Elements into Arabic. This work was twice translated, first under the Khaleefah Harun al-Rasheed (786 – 809 CE) and second under his son al-Ma'mun.

Abu Sa'id al-Darir al-Jurajani (d. 845 CE), who was a Muslim astronomer and mathematician, wrote on geometrical problems.

By the end of the 10th century CE, the number of mathematicians increased immensely Abu Kamil (850 – 930 CE), who was one of the distinguished mathematicians of this period, perfected al-Khwarizmi's work on algebra. He determined and constructed both roots of quadratic equations. He made a special study of the pentagon and decagon with algebraic treatment, mentioned the multiplication and division of algebraic quantities as well, resolved systems of equations up to five unknowns. His work was studied and greatly utilized by al-Karkhi and Leonardo of Pisa.

Abu al-Wafa's contribution to the development of trigonometry is remarkable. He was the first to show the generality of the sine theorem relative to spherical triangles. He gave a new method of constructing sine tables, and calculated the value of sin 30° to eight decimal places.

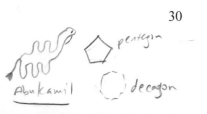

'Umar ibn Ibrahim al-Khayyam was one of the greatest Muslim mathematicians and astronomers of the Middle Ages. While al-Khwarizmi deals only with quadratics, al-Khayyam mostly discusses the cubic equations. He makes a remarkable classification of the equations, which are based on the complexity of the equation, i.e. on the number of different terms which they contain.

The 'Banu Musa' or 'Sons of Musa', wrote a series of important original studies. One title was done by Muhammad ibn Musa ibn Shakir, which dealt with the measurement of the sphere, trisection of the angle, and determination of two mean proportionals to form a single division between two given quantities. His interest was not limited to geometry; he also wrote works on celestial mechanics, the atom, the origin of the Earth and an essay on the Ptolemaic universe. His brother Ahmad ibn Musa ibn Shakir wrote a fundamental work on mechanics, while Al-Hasan ibn Musa ibn Shakir wrote a study of the geometrical properties of the ellipse. Al-Hasan was perhaps the most gifted geometrician of his time. He translated the first six books of Euclid's Elements and left the rest unfinished because he was able to work out the remaining propositions himself.

Another mathematician and geographer was Al-Hasan ibn 'Ali al-Marrakushi, who flourished until 1262 CE. He wrote various works on astronomy, which was put to practical use in astronomical instruments and methods. Also, Abu al-Abbas Ahmad ibn Muhammad ibn 'Uthman al-Azdi, a very popular Muslim writes authored 74 works that dealt with mathematics and astronomy. One of his books, *Talkhis Amal al-Hisab* (Summary of Arithmetical Operations) was studied for at least two centuries. It was highly admired by Ibn Khaldun, and a French translation of it appeared in 1864 CE.

31

Physics and Technology

- Force, Motion and Light
- The Balance
- Al-Khurasani, the Clock Maker
- Hydraulic Apparatus
- Elasticity of Air
- Hammam (Steam Bath)
- Magnetic Needle
- Guns and Cannons
- Science of Optics
- Research in Spherical & Parabolic Mirrors
- Research in Angles of Incidence & Reflection

Muslim scientists studied the fundamental questions of physics deeply. For example Ibn Sina made profound studies of such phenomena as force, motion, light, heat, and vacuums to name a few. A great progress was made in theoretical and applied mechanics. Valuable work was done in the field of mechanics on the wheel, axle, lever pulley, inclined plane windmill, waterwheel, toothed wheel, and other mechanical devices.

The physicist and astronomer al-Khazini wrote a book on mechanics, hydrostatics and physics named *Kitab Mizan al-Hikmah* (Book of the Balance of Wisdom) which is the most remarkable medieval work on these subjects. It gives a theory of the force of the attraction of the Earth (gravity), according to which the universal force is directed towards the center of the universe.

In another book on the balance al-Khazini stresses the need to remove, as far as possible, the influences of temperature variation during weighing. When al-Khazini's other studies are considered, he seems to be a precursor of Galileo.

Before al-Khazini, 'Umar al-Khayyam did the greatest work on the balance. Ibn Sina and al-Razi (d.924 CE) contributed to the theory of the balance. Al-Razi made investigations on gravity by using the hydrostatic balance, than called *Al-Mizan al-Tabi'i* (The Physical Balance).

Muhammad ibn 'Ali ibn Rustam al-Khurasani was a famous constructor of clocks, and as a result, he was called *al-Sa'ati* (the clock maker). Another Muslim mechanic of the 13th century CE was Abu al-'Isa Ismail ibn Razzaz Badi al-Zaman al-Jazari. He wrote a dissertation on the knowledge of the geometrical mechanical contrivance that deals mainly with hydraulic apparatus like fountains. This important work is interesting from the technical point of view, and represents the best Arabic work on applied mechanics. Qaisar ibn Abu al-Qasim, a mathematician and astronomer (d. 1251 CE) made improvements on the waterwheels. Such improved types of water-wheels are still seen on Orontes[7] and are among the glories of Hama.

Abu Nasr al-Farabi refuted the existence of a vacuum. He wrote a remarkable essay on the elasticity of the air. It is an original piece of research.

The Muslims developed the techniques of bathing. They constructed the hot steam bath called Hammam (from the Arabic root *hamm*, meaning to heat).

Muslims were the first to apply the directive property of the magnetic needle in determining their direction while traveling on the sea.

The Muslims were also the first to use explosives material in guns and cannons. The purpose of this invention was to throw bullets at the enemy

---

[7] The Orontes or al-'Asi is a river of Lebanon, Syria and Turkey

from a long distance. The Chinese used sodium nitrate only. But the penetrating power of explosives was discovered and used only by the Muslims. The earliest known military applications of these explosive gunpowder compositions were the explosive cannons first used by the Muslims to repel the Mongols at the Battle of Ain Jalut in 1260 CE.

The statement given by Ibn Khaldun in his *History of Berbers* also proves the use of the guns at the time of war. He writes:

> "Abu Yusuf the Sultan of Morocco besieged the city of Sijilmasa in 1273 CE. He installed the instruments for besieging in front of the city. These instruments consisted of Manjneeq, Urawe and Handam with which the bits of iron were thrown. These bits were filled in the box of Handam, and the explosives kept behind them were set on fire. Its effect was powerful."

Muslims developed the science of optics. Ibn al-Haytham made a remarkable contribution towards this science. Indeed modern optics began with him. He showed remarkable progress in experimental techniques. He made research on spherical and parabolic mirrors and dioptrics. He noticed that the relation between the angles of incidence and reflection does not remain constant. He gave a better description of the eye and vision. He tried to explain binocular vision, and gave a correct explanation of the apparent increase in the size of the sun and the moon near the horizon. Ibn Sina made a deep study of light. He observed that if light is emitted due to the ejection of some sort of particles by the luminous source, the speed of light must be finite. Al-Biruni noticed that the speed of light is immensely greater than that of the sound.

Astronomy

- Need for Astronomical Science
- Travel for Trade
- Find direction of Makkah
- Building Mosques
- Star Maps
- Astrolabes
- Building of Observatories
- Celestial Motions
- Geodetic Measurements
- Verification of Solar Year
- Astronomical Instruments

The Arabs took a keen interest in the study of the heavens. They developed this interest because as the dwellers of the desert who usually traveled at night in connection with trade, war and migration from one place to another, they found the direction of their journey with the help of the stars. The clear sky of the desert gave them a chance of making precise observations. Thus there was some locally acquired knowledge of the fixed stars, the movements of the planets and the changes of the weather. After the advent of Islam, the Muslims had to determine the time of the prayers and the direction of the Ka'abah. For this Muslims who once flourished in trade all over the world of launched Jihad, had to travel on the land and the sea. As an aid to travel, navigation and meteorology, a by-product of navigation, they needed star maps. The necessity of such maps also resulted in their interest in astronomy.

The regular study of astronomy and mathematics was begun at Baghdad in the second half of the 8th century CE during the time of the second 'Abbasi Khaleefah al-Mansur. The investigations on astronomy continued until the end of the 11th century CE. Nearly all of the original and creative work was done by Muslims. Astronomy reached its highest in the 13th and

35

14th centuries CE. In the 12th century CE, the Christians and Jews started the work of translation from Arabic into Latin and Hebrew, and began to conduct research in this field. But until the end of the 13th century CE, no mathematical and astronomical work comparable to that of the Muslims could be produced by the Christians or Jews.

The Muslim astronomers also prepared the star maps to preserve the old astronomical knowledge and to use them as aid to travel navigation and meteorology. Astronomer Ibrahim ibn Habib al-Fazari was the first Muslim who constructed astrolabes. He composed a poem on astrology, and compiled a Zij (calendar) according to the Arab method. He also wrote on the use of astrolabes and on the armillary spheres.

During the time of Khaleefah al-Ma'mun the important work of translation of Ptolemy's Almagest from Greek into Arabic was completed. Khaleefah al-Ma'mun (786-833 CE) built an observatory in Baghdad in his Bayt al-Hikmah and another in the plains of Tadmor[8]. In these observatories the fundamental elements of the Almagest like the inclination of the ecliptic, the length of the solar year, and the precession of the equinoxes were verified. Observations on the celestial motions were carried out and geodetic measurements were made.

More original and improved work was done in the second half of the 10th century CE. The elaboration of trigonometry, which was considered to be a branch of astronomy at that time, was also continued. Great attention was paid to the construction of good astronomical instruments, especially to the spherical astrolabe which was newly introduced at that time. Hamid ibn 'Ali and 'Abdullah Muhammad ibn Jabir ibn Sinan al-Battani were famous makers of astrolabes. Al-Battani is considered to be one of the greatest astronomers of Islam. He carried out astronomical observations of a wide range and with remarkable accuracy for about 41 years (871-9 18

---

[8] Tadmor was a city of central Syria, located 215 km northeast of Damascus and 120 km southwest of the Euphrates.

CE). He determined many astronomical coefficients, like the precession 54.5" a year and the inclination of the ecliptic 23° 35', with great accuracy. He noticed an increase of 16° 47' in the longitude of the sun's apogee since Ptolemy's time.

This led to the discovery of the motion of the solar episodes and of slow variation in the equation of time. Al-Battani proved the possibility of the annular eclipses of the sun. Al-Battani's astronomical work was translated into Latin and Spanish in the 12th and 13th centuries CE respectively. It exerted a great influence on the European scholars of the Middle Ages and Renaissance.

To honor the great achievements of Muslims in the field of astronomy, 24 Moon craters were named after scholars from the Islamic civilization by the International Astronomical Union in 1935, 1970 and 1976 CE.

Na Carbonate | Copper | plaster | Quick
K Carbonate | lead | of paris | lime
| toxic | in surgery | depilatory

Development of Science and Technology in Islamic History

Chemistry

- Definition of Organic and Inorganic Chemistry
- Sulfur Mercury Theory of Metals جابرین حیان
- Calcination جابرین حیان
- Reduction جابرین حیان
- Discoveries of various Acids Sulfuric & Nitric acids
- Preparation of Drugs
- Applied Chemistry → الرازی – using chemical knowledge for medical purposes
- Paper

Chemistry deals with the composition and properties of substances and the changes of composition they undergo. It has been divided into Inorganic and Organic. The conception of this division in modem Chemistry came from al-Razi's classification of chemical substances into mineral, vegetable and animal.

Inorganic Chemistry, which deals with the preparation and properties of the elements and their compounds, originally arose from the study of minerals and metals. Organic chemistry, which deals with carbon compounds, developed through the investigation of animal and plant products.

A Greek philosopher, Empedocles, held the view that all the four elements, air, water, earth and fire, were the primal elements, and that the various substances were made by their intermixing. He regarded them to be distinct and unchangeable. Aristotle considered these elements to be changeable, i.e. one kind of matter could be changed into another kind.

Jabir ibn Hayyan, a great Muslim chemist of the 8th century CE, modified the Aristotelian doctrine of the four elements, and presented the so called

38

sulfur mercury theory of metals. According to this theory, metals duller essentially because of different proportions of sulfur and mercury in them. He also formulated the theory of geologic formation of metals. Unlike his Greek predecessors, he did not merely speculate, but performed experiments to reach certain conclusions. He recognized and stated the importance of experimentation in chemistry. He combined the theoretical knowledge of the Greeks and the practical knowledge of craftsmen, and made noteworthy advances both in the theory and practice of chemistry.

Jabir's contribution to chemistry is very great. He gave a scientific description of two principle operations of chemistry. One of them is calcination which is employed in the extraction of metals from their ores. The other is reduction which is employed in numerous chemical treatments. He improved upon the methods of evaporation, melting, distillation, sublimation and crystallization. These are the fundamental methods employed in the purification of chemical substances, enabling the chemist to study their properties and uses, and to prepare them. The process of distillation is particularly used for taking extracts of plant material.

The most important discovery made by Jabir was the preparation of sulfuric acid. The importance of this discovery can be realized by the fact that in this modern age the extent of the industrial progress of a country is mostly judged by the amount of sulfuric acid used in that country. Another important acid prepared by him was nitric acid which he obtained by distilling a mixture of alum and copper sulfate. Then by dissolving ammonium chloride into this acid, he prepared aqua regia which unlike acids, could dissolve gold in it.

Jabir classified chemical substances, on the basis of some distinctive features, into bodies (gold, silver, etc.) and souls (mercury, sulfur, etc.) to make the study of their properties easier.

In the same century Jabir's work was further advanced by al-Razi who wrote many chemical treatises, and described a number of chemical instruments. He applied his chemical knowledge for medical purposes, thus laying the foundation of applied chemistry.

الومن

Abu Mansur distinguished between sodium carbonate and potassium carbonate. He had some knowledge of arsenious oxide, cupric oxide, antimony and other substances. He knew the toxicological effects of copper and lead compounds, the depilatory virtue of quicklime, the composition of plaster of Paris and its surgical use.

خلف بن عباس الزهروى

The great Muslim surgeon, Khalaf ibn 'Abbas al-Zahrawi wrote a great medical encyclopedia, *Al-Tasrif*, which contains interesting methods of preparing drugs by sublimation and distillation, but it's most important part is the surgical one.

Ibn Sina wrote a treatise on minerals that provided one of the main sources of geological knowledge, and chemistry in Western Europe until the Renaissance.

The Muslim chemists applied their chemical knowledge to a large number of industrial arts. One of them is mentioned here, which will enable the reader to estimate the extent of their knowledge of Applied Chemistry.

Paper is also featured in the pioneering works of the Muslims. Paper was invented by the Chinese who prepared it from the cocoon of the silk worm. Some specimens of Chinese paper dates back to the second century CE. The first manufacture of the paper outside China occurred in Samarqand[9] in 757 CE. When Samarqand was captured by the Muslims, the manufacture of paper spread all over the Muslims World. By the end of the 12th century CE, there were four hundred paper mills in Fas alone. In Spain the main center of manufacturing of paper was Shatiba which

---

[9] Samarkand is the second-largest city in Uzbekistan and the capital of Samarqand Province.

remained a Muslim city until 1239 CE. Cordova was the center of the paper business in Spain.

Unica name

The Muslims developed this art. They prepared paper not only from silk, but also from cotton, rags and wood. In the middle of the 10th century CE the paper industry was introduced into Spain. In Khurasan[10] paper was made from linen. Joseph Karabacek[11], in one of his works, explains the process of making paper in minute detail, describing how the pulp is prepared to make sheets, washed and cleaned them, colored, polished and pasted. No text comparable to this in any other language exists from that time.

The preparation of pulp involves a large number of complicated chemical processes, which indicates the level of achievement in chemistry reached by Muslims.

The manufacture of writing paper in Spain is one of the most beneficial contributions of Muslim to Europe. Without paper the scale on which popular education in Europe developed would not have been possible. The preparation of paper from silk would have been impossible in Europe due to the lack of silk production there.

The Muslims method of producing paper from cotton could only be useful for the Europeans. After Spain the art of paper making was established in Italy in1268 CE. France owed its first paper mills to Muslim Spain. From these countries the industry spread throughout Europe.

---

[10] A region which covered parts of modern day Afghanistan, Tajikistan, Iran, Uzbekistan, and Turkmenistan.
[11] Joseph Karabacek, d. Vienna, 1918, orientalist, professor at the university of Vienna, 1899-1917 director of the court library, together with C. W. Huber founder of the Vienna numismatic association, leading personality in the field of Arabic papyrology.

Medicine

- Translation of Work from Other Languages
- Knowledge of Anatomy
- Physiology
- Bacteriology
- Surgery
- Optical Work
- Operation of Cataracts
- Structure of the Eyes
- Cesarean Operation
- Development of Hospitals
- Mobile Hospitals
- Medical Schools

Centuries before the advent of Islam the Arabs had their own system of medicine in the form of herb and shrubs which was based on Chaldean[12] medicine and on their own experience. Gradually Greek medicine attracted their attention. Harith ibn Kaldah was the first to introduce Greek medicine to the Arabs. Khalid ibn Yazid ibn Mu'awiya had some Greek and Egyptian books translated into Arabic during the 'Umayyah period. But the science of medicine flourished during the time of the Abbasids.

Initially, the Muslims made arrangements for the translation of Greek, Indian, Persian and Chaldean medical works into Arabic, and thus received their knowledge of medicine from these nations. Before they accepted at face value the information they extracted, they conducted research in various branches in medicine to verify what they gathered from these texts.

---

[12] Chaldea, 'the Chaldees' was a Hellenistic designation for a part of Babylonia, which existed in the region of modern Iraq.

In addition, they made many valuable new discoveries in medical theory and practical. By combining their discoveries, with the information they filtered from other sources they evolved an entirely new system of medicine.

The Arabs had a fair knowledge of anatomy as it is obvious from the names of the internal and external organs of the human and animal bodies found in the literature of pre-Islamic Arabia. When they became acquainted with the Greek anatomical descriptions, they made investigations on them, pointed out many errors in the work of their predecessors, and made many new discoveries in this field.

In order to verify the Greek anatomical ideas prevailing at that time, Yuhanna ibn Masawaih made dissections of apes supplied to him by the order of the 'Abbasi Khaleefah Mu'tasim Billah. After this verification he composed his work on anatomy. The works of some Muslim physicians and surgeons, like *Tashrih al-Mansuri* by Mansur ibn Muhammad, contain illustrations of human organs, which are not found in the Greek works. These illustrations also throw light on the Muslims' practical knowledge of anatomy.

In the field of physiology the work of the Muslim physicians is quite valuable. For instance, Ala al-Din Abu al-Hassan 'Ali ibn Abi Hazm al-Qarshi of Damascus explained the theory of the minor circulation of blood three centuries before William Harvey, who is credited with this discovery. Also, al-Qarshi suggested that food is fuel for the maintenance of the body's heat. Abu al-Faraj 'Ali ibn al-Hussein held that there are canals in the nerves through which sensations and movement are transmitted.

The contributions of Muslims in the field of bacteriology are quite revolutionary. According to Browne, Muslims were fully aware of the theory of germs. Ibn Sina was the first to state that bodily secretions are

43

contaminated by foul foreign earthly bodies before getting the infection. Ibn Khatimah of the 14th century CE stated that man is surrounded by minute bodies which enter the human body and cause disease. His observation was made from the great plague that effected many parts of the world. Ibn al-Khatib (1313-1375 CE), a Spanish physician, wrote a treatise called *On the Plague*. His observation was:

> "The existence of contagion is established by experience, investigation, the evidence of the senses and trustworthy reports. These facts constitute a sound argument. The fact of infection becomes clear to the investigator who notices how he who establishes contact with the afflicted gets the disease, whereas he who is not in contact remains safe, and how transmission is affected through garments, vessels and earrings."

Some Muslims also gave new suggestions regarding the treatment of diseases. Abu al-Hassan, the physician of Adud al-Dawlah[13] introduced the process of bleeding as a treatment of cerebral hemorrhage which is often due to blood pressure.

Al-Razi suggested nourishing food for the treatment of general weakness. The Muslim physicians were the first to use the stomach tube for the performance of gastric lavage in the case of gas poisoning. They were fully aware of the principles of opotherapy centuries before Browne Sequard, who is ascribed to discovering this method of treatment.
use of glandular extracts from animals for therapy

Sa'id ibn Bishr ibn 'Abdus suggested light foods and cold producing medicines for the treatment of general paralysis and facial paralysis. Ibn al-Wafid gave emphasis upon the treatment of diseases through food control. They discovered the treatment for epidemic jaundice and suggested a reasonable quantity of opium as a treatment of mania. For epistaxis they

---

[13] Fana Khusrau, the son of Rukn al-Dawlah, was given the title of 'Adud al-Dawlah by the Abbasid caliph in 948 CE when Fana was made amir of Fars (one of the regions of Iran).

44

suggested the pouring of cold water on the head.

In the science of surgery there were also many advancements made by Muslims. They introduced the cauterizing agents in surgery. They were the first to apply the method of cooling to stop the hemorrhage, and suture wounds with silken threads.

It cannot go unnoticed that one of the most famous and eminent figure in Islamic medical field was Ibn Sina. It is said that for a thousand years he has retained his original renown as one of the greatest thinkers and medical scholars in history. His most important medical works are the *Qanun* (Canon) and a treatise on cardiac drugs.

In the 11th century CE Ibn Zuhr gave a complete description of the operation of tracheotomy, which was not mentioned by the Greeks. Abu al-Qasim al-Zahrawi invented many surgical instruments illustrated in his book *Al-Tasrif*. In the same book he described the methods of operations for various diseases. While describing the operations of the skull and its parts, the Muslim surgeons made a mention of operations of the uvula and nasal cavity. They also used methods of tonsillectomy and paracentesis of the ear drum.

The Muslim opticians did valuable and original work in the treatment of eye diseases and surgery. Many of the surgical principles formulated by Muslims are still utilized today. The method of operation of cataracts was first described by them. They knew that cataracts were due to the incapacity of the eye lens. Ibn al-Haytham described the structure of the eye and gave revolutionary ideas regarding the mechanism of sight and describing various types of lenses.

The art of midwifery was highly developed by Muslims. Abu al-Qasim al-Zahrawi invented the method of cranicolsy for the delivery of dead fetus and applied it himself. A book entitled *Al-Athar al-Baqiyyah* in the University of Edinburgh contains an illustration showing an Arab

45

physician performing cesarean operation.

During the time of Banu 'Umayyah rule, the Muslims developed the institution of hospitals. During the time of the 'Abbasi Khaleefah Harun al-Rasheed a hospital was built in Baghdad, which was the first in the history of this city. Many new hospitals were established shortly afterwards. Some of them had their own gardens in which the medicinal plants were cultivated. The large hospitals had medical schools attached to them. Besides such hospital there were a large number of mobile hospitals in the Muslim world.

The Muslim hospitals served as models for the hospitals established in different parts of Europe, particularly in Italy and France during the 14th century CE due to the influence of the Crusades. The Crusaders were inspired by the magnificent hospitals of the Seljuq ruler Nur al-Din in Damascus and those of the Mamluk Sultan al-Mansur Qala'un in Cairo.

Botany and Agriculture

- Names of Plants
- Method of Plantation
- Irrigation and Agricultural Methods
- Simple Drugs

There was a great scarcity of water and vegetation in the deserts of Arabia. The people living there needed plants to feed their animals. They wandered in search of vegetation, and went wherever they could find it. This great importance of plants resulted in their becoming an important topic of Arabic literature.

The study of plants was chiefly made from medical and agricultural point of view The Arabs already knew about the medical use of some herb and shrubs. When Muslims came in contact with other people, they took interest not only in the names and uses of plants, but they also became interested in their cultivation. They sought to understand matters relating to agriculture such as the methods of plantation and fertilization, the suitable times for sowing and harvesting, and the nature of the soil. They made correct observations on sexual differences between such plants as palms and hemp. The plants were classified into those which grew from cuttings and those which grow from seeds.

The Muslims' knowledge of applied botany and agriculture can be estimated by reading the accounts of gardens and crops cultivated in different parts of the Muslim world, particularly those in Spain. At one time Muslim Spain was proverbial in this respect. The Arabs introduced irrigation and agricultural methods that transformed the region into a garden. Cotton, rice, sugar cane, asparagus, oranges, lemons and pomegranates were some of the plants and fruits brought from outside and cultivated in Spain. Throughout the countries the Europeans became aware of the cultivation of many plants which they did not know before.

47

The famous gardens of Persia, Spain and Morocco, with well planned arrangements of trees, shrubs and flowers, with their filled floors, their rivulets and fountains of water built with an aesthetic taste, establishing harmony between architecture and vegetation, throws light on their interest in agriculture, gardening and love for flowers.

Because the Arabs did not know much about the art of agriculture, they turned towards other peoples including the Romans, Nabateans and Persians for learning it. After they acquired this knowledge, they applied it.

In the 8th and 9th centuries CE the land of Iraq had a population of 30 million. Eighty percent of the population consisted of farmers. There were modern irrigation systems from the Tigris and Euphrates. The *kharaj* (land tax) upon irrigated land was 5% versus 10% for land not mechanically irrigated (thereby encouraging agricultural investment). The ratio of yield to seed for wheat in the Muslim world was 10 to 1 compared to 2.5 to 1 in Europe at the time of Charlemagne.

As far as plants themselves are concerned, there were many lexicographers, geographers, travelers and physicians who wrote about them. One of them was 'Abd al-Malik ibn al-Quraib al-Asmai. He was a native of Basrah, and came to Baghdad during the time of Khaleefah Harun al-Rasheed. Asmai was born in 739 or 740 CE and died in 828 CE. He is the author of a number of works on different subjects. One of them is on plants and trees. In the preface of this book the author provided a general discussion on plants. First he mentions various types of soils having different conditions regarding their capabilities for cultivation and vegetation. Then be mentions the trees, giving an account of their various stages of development. Afterwards he classifies the plants, giving examples of each class. Finally, he describes those plants which grow in plains and deserts. He mentions a total of 230 plants in his book.

Al-Biruni also made observations on plants. He discovered that flowers have 3, 4, 5, 6 or 18 petals, and never 7 or 9.

One of the most important Muslim botanists was Rashid al-Din Abu al-Fadi ibn 'Ali al-Suri. He was a great authority on simple drugs, the variety of their names, their properties and uses.

Another botanist was Abu Muhammad 'Abd Allah ibn Ahmad al-Maliki al-Nabati, known as Ibn al-Baytar. He was renowned for identifying the plants by name, species and the places where they grew. He traveled to Asia Minor[14] and some other territories and observed the plants in the places where they grew. Ibn al-Baytar is the author of many works on simple drugs and other subjects. One of them, *Kitab al-Jami fi Adwiyyah al-Mufradah* (Book of Simple Remedies and Food), is mainly based on the works of his Greek and Muslim predecessors, but also contains his personal observations made in different lands. He gave in alphabetical order, the Persian, Latin and Berber names of the simple drugs and also cleared the confusion in the names. He also mentioned their properties and uses.

---

[14] Asia Minor is a region of the ancient world that corresponds roughly to modern day Turkey or the peninsula of its Greek name, Anatolia.

Geography

- Reason for studying Geography
- Vastness of the State
- Prayer Direction
- Hajj
- Earth is Round
- Naval Science
- Drawing of World Map

The Muslims had to travel to distant lands across plains cities, deserts, mountains, rivers and seas during trade, military expedition and the administration of their vast state. Within one hundred years after the advent of Islam, their state stretched from Arabia to India in the East, and Morocco and Spain in the West. In the 10th century CE, the Islamic State comprised the territories of Arabia, Egypt with the entire Northern coast of Africa, nearly the whole of Spain, the islands of Sicily, Greece, some Italian towns, Syria, South East of the Caucasus, Mesopotamia[15] including Iraq, the whole of Modern Persia, Afghanistan, Transoxiana[16], and south west territories of India. Travels in these vast lands and their administration necessitated the accumulation of information on them.

The science of geography is somewhat related to astronomy. Therefore, the study of geography was also motivated by the same incentive as astronomy, which was the need for determination of the direction of the

---

[15] Mesopotamia (from the Greek meaning 'between two rivers') was a cradle of civilization geographically located between the Tigris and Euphrates rivers, largely corresponding to modern day Iraq and western part of Iran.

[16] Transoxiana is the largely obsolete name used for the portion of Central Asia corresponding approximately with modern day Uzbekistan, Tajikistan and southwest Kazakhstan.

al-kati
Askiya - Songhay
dynasty

Ka'abah[17] for the orientation of the mosque and for turning faces towards it during the time of prayer.

Another great factor that motivated the study of geography was the annual Hajj. Before leaving for Hajj, the pilgrims generally collected information on the territories which lay on the way to Makkah. To provide such information many itineraries were from different countries to Makkah were shown. In the early days, the information on various lands and its people was supplied mainly by the trader and travelers. In addition, Muslim traders were very active in those days. They reached as far as China, Russia, Zanjibar and the southern tip of Africa.

A large number of books on geography were produced by Muslim geographers and travelers which were widely studied. There are accounts of Ibn Batutah's travel through African jungle, Al-Bakri wrote about West Africa in 1067 CE, the *Geographical Dictionary* was compiled by Abu al-Fida and Yaqut between 1212-1229 CE and Ibn Fadlallah gives a detailed account of life in Mali in his book *Al-'Umari's Masalik al-Absar fi Mamalik al Amsar* that was written between 1342-1349 CE. Mahmud al-Kati, a famous scholar from Africa, wrote *Kitab al-Fattash* in 1519 CE (which was complete by his son Ibn al-Mukhtar in year 1565 CE), which gives details on the Askiya dynasty of the Muslim rule of Songhay of West Africa. Also, 'Abd al-Rahman al-Sa'di wrote *Tarikh al-Sudan* in 1665 CE that provides valuable information about the region and people of Sudan.

The translations of these books were made into many European languages and for centuries the Europeans acquired the knowledge of the world through these books.

---

[17]

The Ka'aba, located in Makkah, Saudi Arabia, is the holiest place in Islam. The *qibla*, the direction Muslims face during prayer, is the direction from their location on Earth towards the Ka'aba. It is around the Ka'aba that ritual circumambulation is performed by Muslims during the Hajj (pilgrimage) season as well as during the 'Umrah (lesser pilgrimage).

The development of naval technology *navigating* was launched during the time of the second Khaleefah 'Umar ibn al-Khattab, when the Muslims started to build the navy. This navy sailed from the ports in Syria and Egypt. Mu'awiya stationed it in the sea adjacent to Cyprus until this region was opened to Islam in 649 CE. During the time of the third Khaleefah, 'Uthman ibn 'Affan, the Islamic navy defeated the Roman navy which was under the command of the emperor Constantine, son of Heraclius, in the famous battle of Umm as-Sawari (the Mother of Masts) in 654 CE.

Among the well known admirals of the Islamic navy were 'Adullah ibn Abu al-Sarh, who led the battle of Umm as-Sawari, and Ahmad ibn Deenar ibn 'Abdullah who defeated the Roman navy in 856 CE, at the time of the 'Abbasi Khaleefah al-Mutawakkil.

The Muslims opened up the land routes to India, China, Malaysia, and Timbuktu, the trade center of Central African trade, and sent their caravans to the rich lands beyond the Sahara long before the Portuguese reached Cape Verde in 1460 CE. They controlled the sea routes to India, and established trade points along the Eastern coast of Africa, from the Sudan Coast and Socotra to Mombassa, Mozambique, Zanzibar and Madagascar.

The seventh 'Abbasi Khaleefah al-Ma'mun took a keen interest in geography. He appointed seventy scholars to draw a large map of the world. One of these scholars, Ibn Musa al-Khwarizmi, compiled a geographical work called *Rasm al-Ma'mur min al-Bilad* (Description of the Inhabited Lands) which contains the results of the research of these scholars. He made improvements on Ptolemy's geographical work, both in the text and in the maps. He followed Ptolemy in giving the latitudes and longitudes of various places. He also gave the geographical positions of the places which originated after the rise of Islam.

The narrative of a Muslim merchant named Sulaiman who undertook

52

Sudan
Zanzibar
Mozambique
Madagascar

travels to China and to many coast lands of the Indian Ocean appeared in 851 CE. It is the first description of these lands in the Arabic language. It throws light on the commercial relations between the Chinese and Muslims during the first half of the 10th century CE.

Another geographer, botanist, lexicographer and historian named 'Abd Allah ibn 'Abd al-Aziz al-Bakri wrote valuable books on many subjects. The kings of the Spanish territories used to send their books to one another as gifts. One of these books is a geographical work called *Kitab al-Masalik wa'l Mamalik*, written by al-Bakri. It is in the form of an itinerary and contains historical and ethnographic information. In addition, he also composed a geographical dictionary mainly of Arabia.

One of the travelers and geographers of the same period was Abu Hamid al-Gharnati, who was born in Granada in 1080 CE. He traveled from Spain to Sardinia and Sicily, and then to Egypt. He then went to Baghdad, Abhar and Jibal Sakhsin on the upper Volga. He also traveled to Bulgaria, Bashgird and Hungary. He is the author of many geographical works. His descriptions of the foreign countries are largely anecdote. One of his works is entitled *Tuhfat al-Albab wa Nukhbat al-A'ja* (Gift to the hearts and choice of wonders), which provides a description of the world and its inhabitants, natural phenomena of various countries and strange geographic oddities.

Another illustrious scholar of this age and the greatest geographer of the Middle Ages was Abu 'Abd Allah Muhammad ibn Muhammad ibn 'Abd Allah, usually called al-Sharid al-Idrisi. He was also a historian, botanist, traveler, literary scholar and a poet. He was brought up at Cordova where he received his education. Then he undertook long journeys in the Mediterranean region until last he reached Sicily.

Al-Idrisi began to compile his monumental work on the world geography entitled *Kitab al-Rujari* (Roger's book) which was completed in 1154 CE. It is the most comprehensive work ever written on medieval history and geography. It is the best Arabic work on the description of Europe. The later Muslim geographers derived information on Europe from this celebrated work.

A Muslim geographer of the 13th century CE was Abu al-Hasan 'Ali ibn Musa ibn Muhammad al-Maghribi. He was also a historian and a poet. He traveled extensively and visited Egypt, Syria and Iraq. He was the guest of Hulagu II. In 1251 CE during his stay in Baghdad 'Ali ibn Musa visited 36 libraries in that city. He had the knowledge of the mouth of the river Senegal. He gave an account of the northern countries of Europe where white bears are found. He mentioned that Iceland is called the island of white falcons and that the true falcons are found in Denmark.

Timeline of Scientists in Islamic History

622 – 632 Prophetic Period.	This period cover the time when the Messenger of Allah (saw) was the ruler. He (saw) had provided enormous amount of advice on health and medicine, and many excellent books are already available on Prophets' medicine, thus this area is not covered this book.
632 – 661 Sahabah Period	This period covers the rule of the four companions of the Messenger of Allah (saw). There are no known major scientific works, although accounts are available for various technological developments, especially related to military warfare.
661 – 750 'Ummayah Period	This period marks the beginning of systematic development in science and technology. The 'Ummayad rulers began encouraging work in science but it is centuries before fruits of this effort are realized.
750 – 1517 'Abbasi Period	This period is the most significant in terms of scientific development. Most of the major achievements of Muslims came in this period as the State fully endorses scientific policy.
1517 – 1924 'Uthmani Period	Although scientific development continued in the early period of 'Uthmani rule due to the momentum created in the Abbasid period, the decline sets in towards the latter half. Second half of 'Uthmani period witnesses ideological weakness, thus leading to political weakness and final abolishment of the Islamic State in 1924. Ideological weakness led to decline in science and technology.

Birth	Death	Region	Name	Field
	704	Hejaz	Khalid ibn Yazid ibn Mu'awiya	Chemistry
721	815	Iran	Jabir ibn Hayyan	Chemistry
740	828	Iraq	'Abd al-Malik ibn al-Quraib al-Asmai	Zoology, Botany, Animal Husbandry
777	857	Iran	Yuhanna ibn Masawaih (or Masawayh)	Medicine
780	850	Uzbekistan	Muhammad ibn Musa al-Khwarizmi	Mathematics, Astronomy
786	833	Iraq	Al-Hajjaj ibn Yusuf ibn Matar	Mathematics
787	886	Afghanistan	Ja'far ibn Muhammad Abu Ma'shar al-Balkhi	Astronomy
	777	Iran	Abu'l-Fadl Nawbakht	Astronomy
	777	Iraq or Iran	Abu Ishaq Ibrahim ibn Habib ibn Sulaiman ibn Samura ibn Jundab al-Fazari	Astronomy, Mathematics
	796	Iraq or Iran	Abu 'Abdullah Muhammad ibn Ibrahim al-Fazari	Astronomy, Mathematics, Translation
800	873	Iraq	Yaqub ibn Ishaq al-Kindi	Philosophy, Physics, Optics
800	873	Iran	Ja'far Muhammad ibn Musa ibn Shakir	Astronomy, Engineering, Geometry, Physics.
805	873	Iran	Ahmad ibn Musa ibn Shakir	Engineering, Mechanics

808	873	Iraq	Hunayn ibn Ishaq	Medicine, Optics, Translator
810	873	Iran	Al-Hasan ibn Musa ibn Shakir	Engineering, Geometry
	815		Yahya al-Bitriq	Poisons
828	889	Iran	Abu Hanifa Ahmed ibn Dawood al-Dinawari	Mathematics, Linguistics
836	981	Turkey	Thabit ibn Qurrah ibn Marwan	Astronomy, Mechanics
838	870	Iran	Ali ibn Rabban al-Tabari	Medicine, Mathematics
	845	Iran	Abu Sa'id al-Darir al-Jurjani	Astronomy, Mathematics
868	929	Turkey	'Abdullah Muhammad ibn Sinan ibn Jabir al-Battani al-Harrani	Mathematics, Astronomy, Engineering
	867	Uzbekistan	Abu al-Abbas Ahmad ibn Muhammad ibn Kathir al-Farghani	Astronomy, Civil Engineering
865	924	Iran	Abu Bakr Muhammad ibn Zakariya al-Razi	Medicine, Ophthalmology, Chemistry
870	950	Turkistan	Abu Nasr Muhammad ibn al-Farakh al-Farabi	Sociology, Logic, Science, Music
	873	Iraq	Hunayn ibn Ishaq al-'Ibadi	Medicine
850	850	Iraq	Hubaysh ibn al-Hasan al-A'sam al-Dimashqi	Ophthalmology
850	930	Egypt	Abu Kamil Shuja' ibn Aslam ibn Muhammad ibn Shuja	Mathematics
892	892		Yuhanna ibn Bukhtishu'	Medicine

	990	Iran	Abu Hamid Ahmed ibn Mohammed al-Saghani al-Asturlabi	Astronomy
903	986	Iran	'Abd al-Rahman al-Sufi	Astronomy
	912	Palestine	Abu 'Abdullah Muhammad ibn Ahmad ibn Sa'eed al-Tamimi	Chemistry
	923	Iran	Abu al-Abbas al-Fadl ibn Hatim al-Nairizi	Mathematics, Astronomy
930	1030	Iran	Ahmad ibn Muhammad Miskawayh	Medicine, Chemistry
932		Iran	Abu al-Hasan Ahmed ibn Muhammad al-Tabari	Medicine
936	1013	Spain	Abu al-Qasim Khalaf ibn al-'Abbas al-Zahrawi	Surgery, Medicine
940	997	Iran	Abul Wafa Muhammad ibn Muhammad ibn Yahya ibn Ismail al-Buzjani	Mathematics, Astronomy, Geometry
943	969	Iraq	Abu al-Qasim Muhammad ibn Hawqal	Geography
951	1029	Spain	bi 'Abd Allah Muḥammad ibn Hasan, also known as Ibn al-Kattani	Medicine
960		Iraq	Ibn Wahshiyh	Chemistry, Botany
965	1040	Iraq	Abu 'Ali al-Hasan ibn al-Hasan ibn al-Haytham	Physics, Optics, Mathematics
973	1040	Uzbekistan	Abu Raihan Al-Biruni	Astronomy, Mathematics
976			Ahmad ibn Abi al-Ash'ath	Medicine
	977	Iran	Abul Qasim 'Ubaidullah ibn 'Abdullah ibn Khurdad-bih,	Geography

			al-Istakhri	
	980	Palestine	Muḥammad ibn Aḥmad Saʿid al-Tamimi	Medicine
	980	Tunisia	Abu Jaʿfar Ahmad bin Abi Khalid ibn al-Jazzar	Medicine
980	1037	Uzbekistan	Abu ʿAli al-Hussain ibn ʿAbd Allah ibn Sina	Medicine, Philosophy, Mathematics
	990	Iran	Abu Mansur al-Hasan ibn Nuh al-Qumri	Medicine
	994	Iran	ʿAli ibn ʿAbbas al-Majusi	Medicine
997	1075	Spain	ʿAbd al-Karim ibnWafid al-Lakhmi	Medicine, Pharmacology
998	1067	Egypt	Abu al-Hasan Ali ibn Ridwan ibn Ali Jaʿfar al-Misri	Medicine
	1001	Spain	Ibn Tumart al-Maghribi, Abu ʿAli Muḥammad ibn Muḥammad, al-Audalusi al-Maliki	Astrology, Medicine
1002	1002	Spain	Ibn Samajun, Abu Bakr Ḥamid	Medicine
950	1009	Egypt	Abu al-Hasan ʿAli abi Saʾid ʿAbd al-Rahman ibn Ahmad ibn Yunus al-Sadafi al-Misri, also known as ibn Yunus	Astronomy, Mathematics
997	1074	Spain	Ibn al-Wafid	Medicine
First half of 11th C	First half of 11th C	Iraq	Sharaf al-Din ʿAli ibn ʿIsa al-Kahhal	Medicine, Ophthalmology

1010	1094	Spain	Abu 'Ubayd 'Abdallah ibn 'Abd al-Aziz ibn Muhammad al-Bakri	Geography
1019			Al-Hasib Alkarji	Mathematics
	1019	Iran	Abu al-Faraj 'Ali ibn al-Hussein	Medicine
1029	1087	Spain	Abu Ishaq Ibrahim ibn Yahya Al-Zarqali	Astronomy
Mid 12th C	Mid 12th C		Ibrahim ibn Abi Sa'id ibn Ibrahim al-Maghribi al-'Ala'i	Medicine
	1100	Iraq	Abu 'Ali Yahya ibn 'Isa ibn Jazlah	Medicine
	1141	Iran	Muhammad ibn Yusuf Ilaqi	Medicine
1044	1123	Iran	Ghiyath al-Din Abul Fateh 'Umar ibn Ibrahim al-Khayyam	Mathematics, Poetry
	1066	Iraq	Abu al-Hasan al-Mukhtar ibn 'Abdun ibn Butlan	Medicine
	1068	Iran	Abu al-Qasim 'Abd al-Rahman ibn 'Ali ibn Abi Ṣadiq	Medicine
1077			Abul Qasim 'Abdul Rahman ibn 'Ali ibn Ahmad ibn Abi Sadiq al-Nisaburi	Medicine
1080	1170	Spain	Abu Hamid al-Gharnati	Geography
1091	1161	Spain	Abu Marwan ibn Zuhr	Surgery, Medicine
1095			Abu Bakr Muhammad ibn Yahya al-Saigh, also known as Ibn Bajah	Philosophy
1099	1166	Spain	Abu 'Abd Allah Muhammad al-Idrisi	Geography

60

Early 12th C	Early 12th C	Iran	Ahmad ibn Farrukh	Medicine
1105	1185	Spain	Abu Bakr Muhammad ibn 'Abd al-Malik ibn Muhammad ibn Tufail al-Qaisi al-Andalusi, also known as Ibn Tufail	Philosophy, Medicine
1061	1120	Iran	Abu Ismaeel al-Hussain ibn 'Ali ibn Muhammad ibn 'Abdul Samad, also known as al-Tughra'i	Chemistry, Poetry
	1153	Turkey	Abu Naṣr 'Adnan ibn Naṣr 'Aynzarbi	Medicine
1076	1165	Iraq	Abu al-Ḥasan Hibat Allah ibn Tilmidh	Calligraphy, Medicine, Poetry, Theology
	1193		Abu Nasr Sa'id ibn Abi al-Khayr al-Masihi ibn 'Isa al-Mutatabbib	Medicine
	1198	Egypt	Ibn Jumay' al-Isra'ili [or, Ibn Jami'], Abu al-Makarim Hibat Allah	Medicine
2nd half of 12th C	2nd half of 12th C		Abu al-Qasim Muhammad ibn 'Abd Allah al-Ansari	Alchemist
1126	1198	Spain	Abu al-Walid Muhammad ibn Ahmad ibn Muhammad ibn Rushd	Biology, Medicine, Philosophy, Physics
1135	1204	Spain	Abu 'Imran Musa ibn 'Ubayd Allah ibn Maymun al-Qurtubi	Medicine, Philosophy
	1136	Iran	Jurjani, Isma'il ibn Muhammad al-Husayn	Medicine
	1140	Iraq	Al-Badee Al-Astrulabi	Astronomy, Mathematics
1149	1209	Iran	Abu 'Abd Allah Muḥammad ibn 'Umar ibn al-Ḥusayn	Theology, Astrology, Medicine

61

			Fakhr al-Din al-Razi	
	1155		Abdul-al Rahman al-Khazin	Astronomy
1155	1208		'Abd al-'Aziz ibn 'Abd al-Jabbar al-Sulami	Medicine
1164	1164	Syria	'Abd al-Raḥman ibn Naṣr ibn 'Abd Allah Shayzari	Medicine
1165	1240	Spain	Muhyi al-Din ibn al-'Arabi	Astrology, Medicine
1163	1231	Iraq	Muwaffaq al-Din Abu Muhammad ibn Yusuf 'Abd al-Latif al-Baghdadi	Medicine, Geography
1165			Ibn A-Rumiyyah Abul'Abbas	Botany
1173	1243	Syria	Rashid al-Din al-Mansur ibn al-Suri	Botany
1184	1253	Tunisia	Ahmad ibn Yusuf al-Tifashi	Metallurgy, Stones
	1191	Syria	Ibn al-Muṭran (or, Ibn Matran), Muwaffaq al-Din Abu Naṣr As'ad ibn Ilyas	Medicine
1197	1248	Spain	Abu Muhammad 'Abd Allah ibn Ahmad Dhia al-Din ibn al-Baytar	Botany, Medicine, Pharmacology
1201	1274	Iran	Abu Jafar Muhammad ibn Muhammad ibn al-Hasan Nasir al-Din al-Tusi	Astronomy, Geometry
1203	1270	Iraq	Ibn Abi Usaybia	Medicine
1204	1292		'Izz al-Din Abu Isḥaq Ibrahim ibn Muḥammad ibn Ṭarkhan Suwaydi	Medicine

	1204		Al-Hassan al-Murarakishi	Mathematics, Astronomy, Geography
	1204	Morocco	Nur al-Din ibn Ishaq al-Bitruji	Astronomy
	1206	Iraq	Ibn Ismail ibn al-Razzaz al-Jazari	Engineering
	1213	Iraq	Ibn Hubal, Muhadhdhab al-Din 'Ali ibn Ahmad, al-Baghdadi al-Khilati	Medicine
1213	1288	Iraq	Ala al-Din Abu al-Hassan Ali ibn Abi Hazm al-Qarshi al-Dimashqi, also known as Ibn al-Nafis	Anatomy, Medicine
	1221	Afghanistan	Abu Hamid Muhammad 'Ali ibn 'Umar Najib al-Din 'Ali al-Samarqandi	Medicine
	1225	North Africa	Abu al-'Abbas Ahmad ibn 'Ali ibn Yusuf al-Buni	Medicine
1233	1286	Syria	Ibn al-Quff, Abu al-Faraj ibn Muwaffaq al-Din Ya'qub ibn Ishaq	
1236	1311	Iran	Qutb al-Din al-Shirazi	Astronomy, Geography
	1240	Egypt	Ibn Abi al-Bayan, Abu al-Fadl Da'ud al-Isra'ili	Medicine
Mid 12th C	Mid 12th C	Turkmenistan	'Abd al-Rahman al-Khazini	Astronomy, Biology, Chemistry, Mathematics
Mid 12th C	Mid 12th C	Iran	Muhammad ibn 'Ali ibn Rustam al-Khurasani, also known as al-Sa'ati	Engineering
	1248	Egypt	Ibn al-Qifti, 'Ali ibn Yusuf	Medicine
	1253		Ahmad ibn Yusuf al-Tifashi	Hygiene, Chemistry

	1285	Morocco	Shihab al-Din al-Qarafi	Fiqh, Optics
Mid 13th C	Med 13th C		Abu al-Qasim Aḥmad ibn Muḥammad al-'Iraqi al-Simawi	Chemistry
1256	1321	Morocco	Abu al-Abbas Ahmad ibn Muhammad ibn 'Uthman al-Azdi (also know as Ibn al-Banna)	Medicine, Mathematics
	1251		Qaisar ibn Abu al-Qasim	Engineering, Mathematics
	1258	Egypt	Fatḥ al-Din ibn 'Uthman ibn Hibat Allah Qaysi	Medicine
1260	1320	Iran	Kamal al-Din Abu al-Ḥasan Muhammad al-Farisi	Astronomy, Physics
	1262	Morocco	Abu 'Ali al-Ḥasan ibn 'Ali al-Marrakushi	Astronomy, Mathematics
1273	1331	Iraq	Abu Al-fida' Isma'il ibn 'ali Al-malik al-Mu'ayyad Imad al-Din (also known as Abu al-Fida)	Astronomy, Geography
1274	1348	Syria	Abu 'Abd Allah Muḥammad ibn Aḥmad ibn 'Uthman al-Dhahabi	Medicine, History, Theology
	1283	Iran	Zakariya' ibn Muḥammad al-Qazwini	Medicine
1290	1290		Amin al-Din Rashid [al-Din] Vaṭvaṭ	Medicine
Late 13th C	Late 13th C		Shams al-Din Muḥammad ibn Maḥmud Shahrazuri	Medicine
1313	1375	Spain	Ibn al-Khaṭib, Lisan al-Din	Medicine
	1344		Mahmud ibn Muḥammad ibn 'Umar al-Jaghmini	Medicine

Development of Science and Technology in Islamic History

	1348	Egypt	Ibn al-Akfani, Shams al-Din, Muhammad ibn Ibrahim al-Sinjari al-Misri	Ophthalmology, Medicine
Mid13th C	Mid-13th C	Syria	'Ali ibn 'Abd al-'Azim al-Ansari	Medicine
1306			Ibn al-Shater al-Dimashqi	Astronomy, Mathematics
	1327	Syria	Shams al-Din, Muhammad ibn Abi Talib al-Ansari al-Sufi al-Dimashqi	Cosmology, Medicine
1332	1406	Tunisia	Abu Zayd 'Abd al-Rahman ibn Muhammad ibn Khaldun	Demography, Economy, History, Sociology
1334	1334		Mas'ud ibn Muhammad Sijzi	Medicine
	1341		Muhammad ibn Aidamer al-Jildaki	Chemistry
1341	1405	Egypt	Muhammad ibn Musá al-Damiri	Zoology
	1342	Iran	al-Jaldaki, 'Izz al-Din Aydamir ibn 'Abd Allah	Alchemist
1351			Abu Abbas ibn Tanbugha ibn al-Majdi	Mathematics, Astronomy
	1357		Kazaruni, Sadid al-Din Muhammad ibn Mas'ud	
	1379		Jamal al-Din Muhammad ibn Muhammad Aqsara'i	Medicine
1380	1429	Iran	Ghiyaseddin Jamsheed Kashani (also known as al-Kashi)	Astronomy, Mathematics
1394	1449	Uzbekistan	Muhammed Taragai Ulugh Beg	Astronomy, Mathematics

	1403		Zayn al-Din 'Ali ibn Husayn al-Ansari, known as Hajji Zayn al-'Attar	
2nd half of 14th C	2nd half of 14th C	Egypt	Shadhili, Sadaqah ibn Ibrahim al-Hanafi al-Misri	Ophthalmology
1410	1453	Egypt	Ibn Shahin al-Zahiri, Ghars al-Din Khalil	Medicine
	1412		Muhammad al-Mahdawi ibn 'Ali ibn Ibrahim al-Sanawbari	Medicine
Mid-14th C	Mid-14th C	Iran	Muhammad ibn Mahmud Amuli	Medicine
	1413		'Ali ibn 'Abd Allah ibn Haydur	Medicine
1427	1427		Husayn ibn Muhammad ibn 'Ali Astarabadhi	Medicine
1445	1505	Egypt	Jalal al-Din Suyuti	Biography, Fiqh, History, Sciences
1448	1517	Egypt	al-Qastallani, Ahmad ibn Muhammad ibn Abi Bakr	Medicine, Judiciary
	1454	Turkey	'Abd al-Rahman ibn Muhammad ibn 'Ali ibn Ahmad al-Bistami	Medicine
1474	1474	Iran	Ghiyath al-Din 'Ali ibn Amiran al-Husayni al-Isfahani	Anatomy, Botany, Meteorology, Mineralogy,
1492	1492	Afghanistan	Muhammad ibn Yusuf Harawi	Medicine
1495	1561	Iraq	Abu al-Khayr ibn Muslih al-Din Mustafá Tashköprüzade	Medicine
Mid 15th C	Mid 15th C	Iran	Imad al-Din Mahmud ibn Mas'ud Shirazi	Medicine

	1520		Muḥammad ibn Muḥammad (Quṣunizade) Qawṣuni	Medicine
1525	1585	Egypt	Taqi al-Din Muḥammad ibn Maʿruf al-Shami al-Asadi	Medicine
1546	1546		Sayyid ʿAli Hamdani	Medicine
	1565	Egypt	ʿAbd al-Wahhab ibn Aḥmad Shaʿrani	Medicine
Mid-16th C	Mid-16th C		Rustam Jurjani	Medicine
	After 1572		Muḥammad ʿAbd Allah ibn Muḥammad ibn Masʿud al-Darʿi al-Tafjaruti (or Tamakruti)	Hygiene
1592	1592		Ḥusayn ibn Ibrahim ibn Wali ibn Naṣr ibn Ḥusayn al-Ḥanafi	Astrology, Medicine
	1599	Syria	Da'ud ibn ʿUmar Antaki	Medicine
1609	1640	Turkey	Hezarfen Ahmet Celebi	Flight, Rocketry
	1609	Iran	Hakim ʿAli ibn Kamal al-Din Muḥammad al-Jilani	Medicine
1600	1600		Muhammad Baqir Yazdi	Mathematics
Mid 17th c	Mid 17th c		Nur al-Din Muḥammad ʿAbd Allah ibn Ḥakim ʿAyn al-Mulk Qurayshi Shirazi	
	1659		Shihab al-Din Aḥmad ibn Aḥmad ibn Salamah al-Qalyubi	Medicine
	1669	Syria	Ibn Sallum, Ṣaliḥ ibn Naṣr	Alchemist, Medicine

1670	1747	Iran	Ḥakim Muḥammad Hashim ibn Ḥakim Muḥammad Hadi Qalandar ibn Muzaffar al-Din ʿAlavi Shirazi	Medicine
1689	1778		Aḥmad ibn ʿAbd al-Munʿim Damanhuri	Medicine
1692	1694	Iran	Qiwam al-Din Muḥammad al-Ḥasani	Poetry on medicine, astronomy, arithmetic, calligraphy
1698	1698		ʿAbd al-Muʿṭi ibn Salim ibn ʿUmar al-Shibli al-Simillawi	Fiqh, Medicine
Late 17th C	Late 17th C		Muḥammad Muʾmin ibn Mir Muḥammad Zaman Daylami Tunakabuni	Fiqh, Medicine
Before 1709	Before 1709		Sulayman ibn Sulayman Muḥammad Karim ibn Muḥammad Wali ibn Ḥajji Himmat ibn ʿIsá ibn Ḥasan	Medicine
1750	1799	India	Tipu Sultan	Rocketry
	1777		Muḥammad ibn Muḥammad, Mufti al-ḥanafiyah bi-al-Quds al-Tafilati	Jurisprudence, Medicine
18th C	18th C		Bulus ibn Qusṭanṭin al-Malaki Shaburi	Medicin
Mid-18th C	Mid-18th C	Egypt	Muḥammad Aqkirmani	Medicine
	1805	India	Ḥakim Muḥammad Sharif Khan	Medicine
Before 1826	Before 1826	Iran	ʿAbd Allah ibn Aḥmad ibn Muḥammad Asfaraʾni	Medicine
1828	1828	Iran	Jalal al-Din Muḥammad al-Iṣfahani	Medicine

68

End of 19th C	End of 19th C		Aḥmad ibn Muḥammad Salawi	Medicine

Decline in Science and Technology

When Islam was being applied as an ideology, with its own political, economic, social, educational and judicial system, Muslims and non-Muslims in the Islamic State enjoyed peace and security, and an environment was created that allowed unhindered scientific discovery. The Islamic State provided finance and support for development of science and technology; it established colleges, universities, research centers and brought together the best minds. This provided the spark that led to the remarkable discoveries and inventions. Thus, development of science and technology was encouraged through state policy and the Muslims rapidly became leaders in many fields of science and technology as a result.

The decline of science and technology in the Muslim world came about as a result of decline in adherence to Islam as an ideology. This ideological decline can be attributed to:

- Infusion of philosophical ideas from Greek, Persian and Indian civilizations
- Abandoned of *ijtihad*[18]
- Neglect of study and understanding of Arabic language
- Missionary, cultural and political invasions of the West

يس

معازب بن جبل

إِجْتِهَاد

(Ijtihad)

---

[18] A process to extract ruling for new problems based on the sources of Islam, the primary sources being the Qur'an and the Sunnah of Prophet Muhammad (saw).

(Khilafa Rashidoon) الخلافة الراشدون

Development of Science and Technology in Islamic History

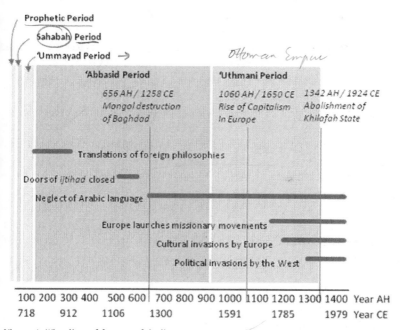

Figure 1: Timeline of factors of decline

Amongst the books translated into Arabic from Greeks, Persians and Indians were the books on philosophies. Some of the ideas of these foreign philosophies took root amongst the Muslim scholars and this caused much confusion in their thinking. These ideas included discussion of whether man is compelled to act or he has free will, the knowledge and attributes of God, spirituality and the dichotomy between the soul and the body. The net result was that efforts were made to reconcile Islam with these philosophies despite complete contradictions between them, thus wrong interpretations and explanations were given.

In the 11th Century CE, the doors of *ijtihad* were closed in the Islamic State. Reasons vary but widespread opinion is that the scholars deemed that all the essential questions have been thoroughly discussed and settled,

71

and there would be no new situations where *ijtihad* will be required. Another reason cited is that this period saw lots of turmoil, with Crusades taking place and Mongols knocking on the doors of the State, and it was felt necessary to stop internal discussions and debates. Whatever the reasons, the abandonment of *ijtihad* stifled thinking and reduced Islamic nation's ability to extract rules to solve new problems. The effect of this could be felt even to the last days of the 'Uthmani rule, where fatwa's[19] were given against using the telephone, citing that it was linked to the whispers of Shaytan (Satan), and printing of the Qur'an was forbidden. Incorrect *ijtihad*, or no *ijtihad*, led Muslims to doubt Islam as they could not see how Islam will solve their practical problems. This led to calls for reforming Islam, thus contributing further towards the ideological decline.

After the destruction of Baghdad in 1258 CE by Mongols, the center of power of the Islamic State shifted to Egypt. However, the key control of the State was in the hands of Mamluks, who were non-Arab in origin. Under their authority, the Arabic language was ignored both in understanding and carrying Islam. The neglect of the Arabic language continued under the 'Uthmani rulers, who took over from the Mamluks in 1517 CE. They too, like the Mamluks, concentrated their efforts on military conquests and neglected the Arabic language despite the fact that it is essential in order to understand Islam and one of the conditions necessary in order to perform *ijtihad*. The neglect of the Arabic language contributed towards the decline in intellectual and legislative aspect of Islam.

The last 300 years also witnessed many campaigns by the West to infiltrate the Islamic State in order to weaken it from within. Military campaigns were initially ruled out as they never proved effective against the Muslims, so they resorted to subtle means. Thus missionaries were sent, beginning in the 17th century CE, to create strife amongst the Muslims by sowing seeds of nationalism. These campaigns eventually succeeded to give away

---

[19] Fatwa is a ruling on Islamic law issued by an Islamic scholar. → actually mufti

to the next phase of political invasions during the 19th century CE, where many parts of Islamic lands were directly occupied. Once the dismantlement of the State was complete in 1924 CE, the West continued with cultural invasion where the secular Western way of life has been pushed on the Muslims.

The above mentioned factors all contributed towards the ideological decline, which blured the vision of the people as the objective of their existence becomes unclear, their priorities of life changed and they faced internal upheavals and conflicts. In fact, ideological decline led to weakness of all institutions of the state initially, but this unchecked decline ultimately led to the destruction of the nation.

The results of the factors of decline only became visible towards the end of 'Uthmani rule when Capitalism emerged in Europe. The rulers were unable to crystallize the nature of the problem facing the nation, because they too were affected by the decline, and thus their incomprehensibility led to the further problems. The Muslims were faced with all sorts of problems internally and externally with the threat from Europe and Russia. Science and technology was amongst the areas directly impacted as the priorities of the State changed towards survival, funding for research and development declined as financial problem became acute and political instability rendered long terms plans futile as nationalism began to take root amongst the Muslims.

Reviving the development of Science and Technology

Can the Muslim world revive its past glory of leadership in science and technology? The answer is yes. The only way Muslims can take this leadership is to go back to what gave them the leadership in the first place. This is the comprehensive adherence to Islam as an ideology, i.e. full acceptance of the Islamic belief and complete implementation of all systems of Islam, as this will create the correct framework for development. Furthermore, the vast intellectual strength and material resources in the Muslim world can only be utilized effectively if the Muslims are united under a single system, as was the case in the past. This unification of Muslims into a single entity is an essential element for success in the advancement of science and technology.

No nation can progress, scientifically or otherwise, if it does not adopt an ideology, and the Muslims are no exception to this rule. The West adopted Capitalism and progress was made in many areas of life as a result. The East was forced to adopt Communism and it also achieved a certain amount of material progress, especially in science and technology. The Muslims have Islam as an ideology and it is this that will provide the basis of progress. Islam provided ideal environment for scientific discovery in the past, and it can do the same again.

In order to succeed, the Muslims have to create an environment for scientific study and research like the one that existed in the past, with a clear vision and strategy, driven from the State apparatus. Proper resources need to be allocated to colleges, universities and research centers. Solving technical problems, improving efficiency of industrial processes, finding cures for diseases and enhancing material life as much as possible should be amongst the objectives in the policy for science and technology. Ideas turned into practical applications to improve the lives of people must be encouraged.

74

Conclusion

An objective observer will notice that science stagnated under the Christian Church in Europe because man had tampered with the original revelation, and the Bible was not meant as the everlasting revelation, but rather for the people of that time. It therefore became impossible to reconcile Christianity with reality. However, science bloomed under Islam as there is no contradiction between science and Islam. Thus, the Muslim world enjoyed its golden period when Europe was steeped in the Dark Ages. Since Islam was kept in its original form, it continued to be applicable for every time and place.

Very little is revealed about the glorious history of Islam, in particular, not much is mentioned about 1000 years of rich scientific heritage of the Muslims, which formed bridge between the ancient Greek, Persian and Indian civilizations with the modern age. Europe inherited much of the scientific heritage of the Muslims when the Islamic influence declined and used that as a foundation of its own scientific revolution.

The Muslims were true pioneers, they established various disciplines of science, they named the stars, and they traveled throughout the world and produced some of the finest thinkers of all time. Household words like chemistry, algebra, aorta, pancreas, camera, sugar, syrup, zero, alkali, cotton, coffee and earth are a living testimony of the everlasting Islamic scientific legacy.

People from different nations and cultures were molded by Islam into a society in which the life, honor, and property of every citizen, Muslim and non-Muslim, was secure. Furthermore, Islam broke the shackles of ignorance that had engulfed humanity and provided a system in which Muslims and non-Muslims excelled, among other things, in science and technology.

Appendix I

Topical lists of European/Latin words with Arabic origins

Some of the popular words used in the field of science have their roots in Arabic.

Names of Stars

English/Latin Name	Arabic Name
Achernar	Akhir al-Nahr
Acrab	Aqrab (Scorpion)
Aega	Nasr al-Waqi
Aldebaran	ad-Dabaran
Altair	Nasr al-Tair
Daneb	Dhanab al-Dujajah
Denebola	Dhanab al-Asad
Fomal Haut	Famm al-Hut
Phurked	Farqad (calf)

Mathematical Vocabulary

English/Latin Name	Arabic Name
Algebra	al-Jabr
Algorism, Algorithm	Al-Khwarizmi
Atlas	Atlas
Average	Awariya
Azimuth	Al-sumut
Cipher, Zero	Sifr
Nadir	Nadir, Nazir
Zenith	Cenit

Development of Science and Technology in Islamic History

Anatomical Terms

Anatomical Terms

English/Latin Name	Arabic Name
Aorta	Avarta
Basilie	Baslik
Cephallie	Kifal
Colon	Colon
Corn	Corn
Cornea	Cornea
Diaphragm	Dayafergma
Epidemis	Aghadidus
Menniges	Mennigies
Mesentry	Masarike
Pancreas	Bankras
Peritoneum	Baratene
Sephenous	Safan
Trochanter	Tracanter

Medical Terms

Medical Terms

English/Latin Name	Arabic Name
Alcanfor, Camphor	Kafur
Alchemy, Chemistry	Al-kimiya
Alcohol	al-khul
Anima	Kitab al-Nafs
Antimonio, Antimony, Antimun	Antimun, Ithmid
Benzene	Luban-Jawi
Colliget	Al-Kullyat
Elixir	al-Aksir
Sufficientia	Kitab al-Shifa
Zircon	Azraq

مكتبة

Maktabah

Names in Chemistry

English/Latin Name	Arabic Name
Adobe	Al-Tub
Alcove	Al-Qubba
Alembic	Alembic
Alkali	Alkali
Aludel	Aludel
Alum	Alum
Amber	Anbar
Arsenal	Dar al-Sina'ah
Artichoke	Al-Kharshuf
Athomor	Athomor
Azymum	Azymum

Other Frequently Used Words

English/Latin Name	Arabic Name
Admiral	Amir al-Bahr
Almanac	Al-Manakh
Amber	Anbar
Arsenal	Dar al-Sina'ah
Artichoke	Al-Kharshuf
Assassin	Hashashin
Athomor	Athomor
Azymum	Azymum
Banana	Banan
Cable	Habl
Calibre	Qalaba
Camel	Jamel
Camera	Qamaara
Canon	Qanun
Checkmate	Shah Mat

Cinnabar	Cinnabar
Cipher	Sifr
Coffee	Qahwa
Cotton	Qutun
Earth	Ardh, Earz
Gibberish	Jabir ibn Hayyan
Giraffe	Zurafa
Hazard	Al-Zahr
Jasmine	Yasmin
Jumper	Jubbah
Lemon	Limun
Lute	Al-'ud
Magazine	Makhazin
Mattress	Matra
Monsoon	Mawsim
Musk	Musk
Orange	Naranj
Rice	Ruzz
Safari	Safara
Safron	Za'faran
Sugar	Sukkar
Syrup	Shurb, Sharab
Tutia	Tutia
Usefur	Usefur
Ziniar	Ziniar

Made in the USA
Columbia, SC
16 September 2017